# It's Fun to Draw Dinosaurs

Mark Bergin

WINDMILL
BOOKS
New York

Published in 2012 by Windmill Books, LLC
303 Park Avenue South, Suite #1280, New York, NY 10010-3657

*Editor:* Rob Walker
*U.S. Editor:* Sara Antill


Library of Congress Cataloging-in-Publication Data

Bergin, Mark.
  Dinosaurs / by Mark Bergin. — 1st ed.
      p. cm. — (It's fun to draw)
  Includes index.
  ISBN 978-1-61533-349-3 (library binding)
  1.  Dinosaurs in art—Juvenile literature. 2.  Drawing—Technique—Juvenile literature.  I. Title.
  NC780.5.B465 2012
  743.6—dc22
                                    2011000107


Manufactured in China

CPSIA Compliance Information: Batch #SS1102WM:
For Further Information contact Windmill Books, New York, New York at 1-866-478-0556

# Contents

# Diplodocus

Di-PLOD-ih-kuss

**1** Start with the head.

**2** Add a dot for the eye and two leaves.

**3** Draw two lines for the neck.

**4** Draw an oval shape for the body.

## Splat-a-Fact

Diplodocus had the longest tail of any animal that has ever walked on Earth.

**6** Draw two long lines for a tail.

## Splat-a-Fact

Fifteen tall men lying end-to-end in a line would measure the same length as a diplodocus.

**5** Draw four legs.

5

# Tyrannosaurus Rex

ti-ran-oh-SOR-us REKS

**1** Draw a rectangle with a half circle.

**2** Draw a smaller rectangle and another half circle.

**3** Draw dots for a nose and an eye, add zigzag lines for teeth.

**4** Add lines for the body.

**5** Draw the arms and the legs.

## You Can Do It!

Paint the tyrannosaurus green. Then draw lines with a yellow wax crayon. Color in with a felt-tip pen or paint. The wax crayon acts as a resistant to the paint.

## Splat-a-Fact

"Tyrannosaurus rex" means "tyrant lizard king." A large meat eater, tyrannosaurus ate large dinosaurs like triceratops.

# Ankylosaurus
an-kuh-lo-SOR-us

**1** Start with the head and eye.

**2** Add a mouth, a nostril, and three spikes.

**3** Draw a big oval shape for the body.

## You Can Do It!

Use a felt-tip pen for the lines and then add color with watercolor paints. Use a sponge to dab on more color for added texture.

**4** Draw two lines for the tail, with small ovals at the end.

## Splat-a-Fact

The ankylosaurus could swing its big, bony tail to club its enemies.

**5** Draw four legs.

**6** Draw a line through the middle of the body.

**7** Add spikes.

8

9

# Pteranodon tuh-RAN-oh-don

**1** Start with the head.

**2** Add a tongue and a dot for the eye.

**3** Draw two lines for the neck and a circle for the body.

**4** Draw the curved shape of the wings.

### Splat-a-Fact

A pteranodon's wings, made of leathery skin, were as large as a hang glider.

**5** Add the legs and the feet.

### You Can Do It!

Use a soft pencil for the lines and add color with watercolor paint.

10

# Dimetrodon
di-MEH-truh-don

**1** Start with the head.

**2** Add the mouth, a nostril, and a circle with a dot for the eye.

**5** Draw a big, curved shape with straight lines in it.

**3** Draw two lines for the neck, joined to a big oval.

**4** Draw two lines to add the tail.

## Splat-a-Fact
A dimetrodon's back sail was made of tough skin and long bones.

**6** Add four legs.

12

13

# Parasaurolophus

pa-ruh-saw-RAWL-uh-fus

**1** Start with the head. Add a small mouth and a dot for the eye.

**2** Draw two lines for a crest. Add nostrils.

**3** Draw two lines for the neck, an oval shape for the body, and two curved lines for the tail.

## You Can Do It!
Paint the parasaurolophus yellow and pink. Then scribble lines with a yellow wax crayon. Add color with paint. The wax acts as a resistant to the paint.

## Splat-a-Fact
Parasaurolophus had the biggest head crest of all the duck-billed dinosaurs.

**4** Draw two legs and two arms

14

15

# Pachycephalosaurus

pak-ee-SEF-ah-lo-sor-us

**1** Start with a head and an eye.

**2** Add the mouth, a nostril, two nose spikes, and some small circles.

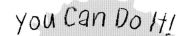

**3** Draw the neck and a big oval for the body. Add two curved lines for the tail and two arms.

## Splat-a-Fact

A pachycephalosaurus was taller than a bus when it stood upright to feed.

## You Can Do It!

Use a felt-tip pen for the lines and add color with chalky pastels. Use your finger to smudge the colors.

**4** Add two legs with clawed feet.

# stegosaurus

steh-guh-SOR-us

**1** Start with the head.

**2** Draw the mouth. Add dots for the nostrils and eye.

**3** Draw two lines for the neck and a circle for the body.

**4** Draw two lines for the tail and add four legs.

**You Can Do It!**
Use felt-tip pens for the lines and add color with wax crayons. Use different kinds of scribbly crayon marks to add variety.

**5** Add kite-shaped plates on its back and spikes at the end of the tail.

**Splat-a-Fact**
Some of the stegosaurus's back plates were about 2 feet (61 cm) tall and 2 feet (61 cm) wide.

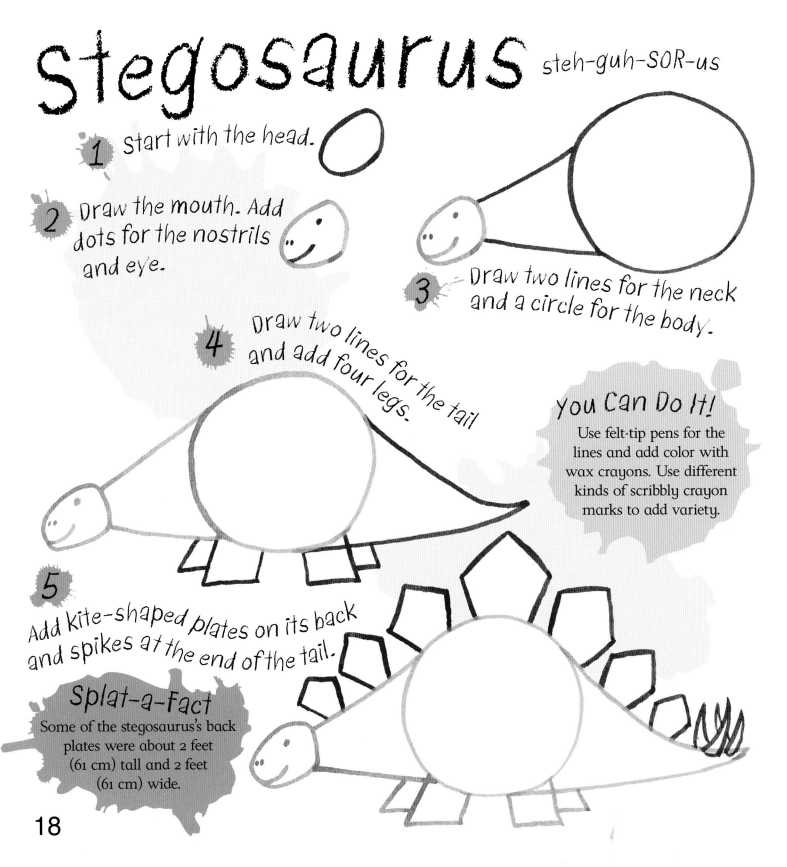

18

19

# iguanodon

ih-GWAH-nuh-don

**1** Start with the head.

**2** Add the mouth and dots for the eye and nostril.

**3** Draw lines for the neck and an oval shape for the body.

**4** Draw two lines for the tail.

**5** Add two legs, two feet, and two arms.

## Splat-a-Fact

The iguanadon was first found in England.

## You Can Do It!

Use a felt-tip pen for the lines and add color with watercolor paints. Make a smudged effect by adding green paint to the yellow while it is still wet.

# Liopleurodon

*ly-uh-PLOR-uh-don*

**1** Cut out the shape of the head.

**2** Draw the eye, nostril, and zigzag mouth.

## you Can Do It!

Cut out the shapes from colored paper with wax crayon stripes. Stick these on a sheet of blue paper. Use a felt-tip pen for the lines and white paint for the air bubbles.

**3** Cut out an oval shape for the body and a pointed tail.

**4** Cut out four pointed flippers.

Make sure you get an adult to help you when using scissors.

## Splat-a-Fact

Liopleurodon had strong flippers to speed through water after its prey.

**5** Glue all of the body into place. Add the head last to overlap.

22

# styracosaurus

stih-RAK-oh-SOR-us

**1** Start with the head. Add spikes, a horn, an eye, and a mouth.

**2** Draw a circle for the body.

## Splat-a-Fact

"Styracosaurus" means "spiked lizard."

**3** Draw two curved lines for the tail.

## You Can Do It!

Use a felt-tip pen for the lines and color in with oil pastels. Smudge colors together with your finger.

**4** Add four legs.

24

# Velociraptor

veh-LAWS-uh-rap-tur

**1** Start with the head. Add a dot for the eye.

**2** Add the nostril, mouth, and teeth.

**3** Draw two lines for the neck and an oval shape for the body.

**4** Draw two lines for the tail and two arms.

**You Can Do It!**
Use a felt-tip pen for the lines and add color using colored pencils.

**Splat-a-Fact**
Velociraptors starred in the film *Jurassic Park*.

**5** Add two legs with clawed feet.

# Triceratops try-SER-uh-tops

**1** Start with the head and add a dot for the eye.

**2** Draw three horns and the mouth.

## You Can Do It!

Use a felt-tip pen for the lines. Add color with watercolors or ink. Use a wax crayon, then paint on top. The wax will act as a resistant. Make a smudge on the triceratops by adding orange paint to the pink paint while it is still wet.

**3** Draw an oval shape for the body.

## Splat-a-Fact

A triceratops was almost twice the length of today's rhinoceros.

**4** Add four legs and draw two curved lines for the tail.

28

# Corythosaurus
koh-RITH-oh-sor-us

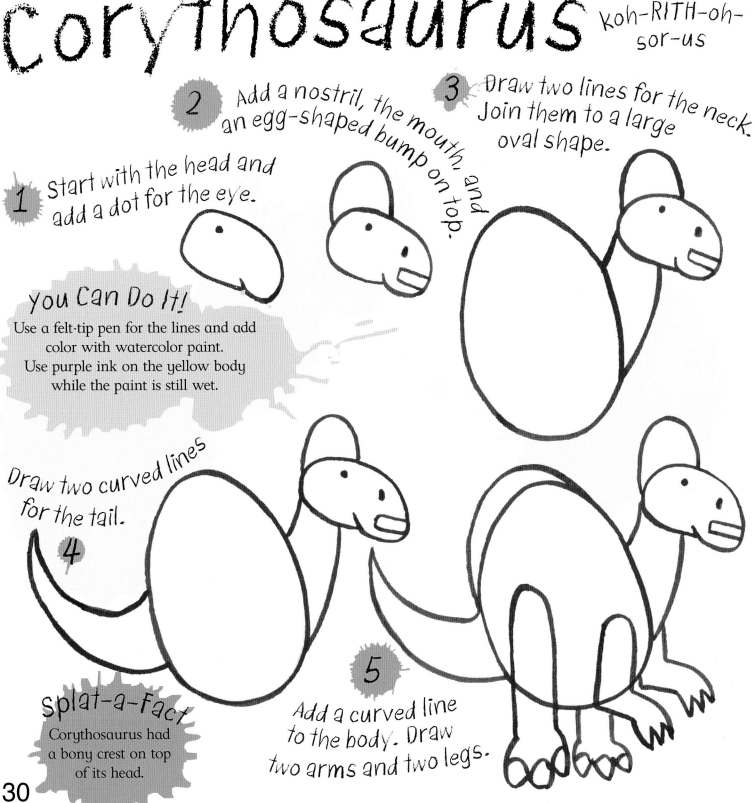

**2** Add a nostril, the mouth, and an egg-shaped bump on top.

**3** Draw two lines for the neck. Join them to a large oval shape.

**1** Start with the head and add a dot for the eye.

### You Can Do It!
Use a felt-tip pen for the lines and add color with watercolor paint. Use purple ink on the yellow body while the paint is still wet.

Draw two curved lines for the tail.
**4**

### Splat-a-Fact
Corythosaurus had a bony crest on top of its head.

**5** Add a curved line to the body. Draw two arms and two legs.

31

# Read More

Harpster, Steve. *Dinosaurs*. Pencil, Paper, Draw!. New York: Sterling Publishing, 2006.

Lessem, Don. *National Geographic Kids Ultimate Dinopedia: The Most Complete Dinosaur Reference Ever*. Des Moines, IA: National Geographic Children's Books, 2010.

Mehling, Carl. *Giant Meat-Eating Dinosaurs*. Discovering Dinosaurs. New York: Windmill Books, 2010.

# Glossary

**crest** (KREST)  A head decoration on an animal.

**flippers** (FLIH-perz)  Wide, flat body parts that help animals swim.

**nostril** (NOS-trul)  One of the openings to the nose.

**prey** (PRAY)  An animal that is hunted by another animal for food.

**resistant** (rih-ZIS-tent) Something that is not affected by something else.

**smudge** (SMUJ)  To blend together.

# Index

# Web Sites

For Web resources related to the subject of this book,
go to: www.windmillbooks.com/weblinks and select this book's title.